AGENCYMAXX MARKETING

Marlin Bollinger

authorHOUSE®

AuthorHouse™
1663 Liberty Drive
Bloomington, IN 47403
www.authorhouse.com
Phone: 1 (800) 839-8640

Published by AuthorHouse 01/23/2017

ISBN: 978-1-5246-6072-7 (sc)
ISBN: 978-1-5246-6077-2 (e)

Library of Congress Control Number: 2017900934

Print information available on the last page.

Any people depicted in stock imagery provided by Thinkstock are models, and such images are being used for illustrative purposes only.
Certain stock imagery © Thinkstock.

This book is printed on acid-free paper.

Dedication

The content of this book and the marketing efforts of The Bollinger Companies would not be possible without the efforts and guidance of my entire staff: Greg Adams, Lorraine Anderson, Stan Brooks, Jeffrey Dressel, CLU, ChFC, Ann Favata, Victor Grieco, Evelyn Martinez, Tere Rizzo, Gregg Simonsen, Jerisma Stubbs, Bridgette Wildgoose, Peter Wilson, and Andrew Yska.

Contents

Contents

Preface

In 2011, I wrote a book entitled "Cross-Marketing, Here's Your Wake Up Call". The book is a chronology of my insurance career and the marketing concepts I learned while working with property/casualty agencies. When the book was formally reviewed, I was criticized for two things: utilizing only a handful of resources and the simplicity of my marketing ideas. At first, I was frustrated by the reviewer's comments, only to finally realize that he had paid me a compliment.

Anyone that has worked with property/casualty agencies related to financial services cross-marketing will be quick to inform you that little research material is available on the subject. Furthermore, many of the articles available are ones that, I either wrote, or was part of a formal interview process. Having worked with property/casualty agencies for more than 35 years has provided me with a thorough understanding of simple, cost effective, marketing programs that really work. The world of insurance marketing, regardless of the discipline, is a dynamic world requiring constant changes to stay abreast of new concepts, products, and technology.

"AgencyMaxx Marketing" is the most comprehensive turnkey cross-marketing system we have ever developed. Although the system is quite detailed, we are proud of its simplicity of execution, proactive approach, and proven profitability. Welcome to "AGENCYMAXX MARKETING".

CHAPTER 1

Status Quo

Property/casualty agencies often struggle when attempting to offer genres of business other than personal and commercial lines. I'm specifically referring to individual life, annuity, and related products. Although many property/casualty agents are properly licensed to sell these products, their conceptual and product knowledge is extremely limited. Any life insurance they do sell is typically term insurance, the most simple and easiest product to explain. Unfortunately, term insurance may not always provide the most appropriate solution for their client.

If the property/casualty agent does not have a working lexicon of financial services terms, he or she will certainly not be anxious to broach the subject with agency clientele. Therefore, the marketing of life and annuity products is almost always reactive in nature. The result is a massive loss of potential agency revenue. That fact alone is not enough to convince an agency principal to seriously consider financial services cross-marketing.

With the reduction in commissions and contingencies, as well as increased costs associated with technology, many agencies would welcome the addition of financial services revenues, if only they knew how easy it is to make it happen. In addition to being somewhat naïve, agencies are consumed with the everyday task of managing their present book of business and don't have time to cross-market life and annuity products. Or so they think.

In 1997, Robert S. Littell, CLU, ChFC, FLMI and Larry McSpadden, CPCU, ARM published a book entitled *"Crossing the Line", Sales Strategies for Life & Health in the P&C Agency.*[1] As an experienced life and health producer and property/casualty cross-marketing consultant, I carefully critiqued the publication. I commend Misters Littell and McSpadden for their comprehensive approach to cross-marketing. In fact, there was so much information, I fear it may discourage an agency from entering the cross-marketing arena all together. I agree with almost every tidbit of advice they provide, as they thoroughly cover every aspect of cross-marketing, including historical data, agency makeup, psychological differences between the two disciplines, and the extent of strategic planning necessary to succeed. Many of their topics mirror my thoughts and experience, providing the need and justification for the AgencyMaxx marketing system. Where they instruct the agency in what to do, when to do it, and how to do it, AgencyMaxx provides a platform to do it for them.

The first step in financial services cross-marketing is not product and concept knowledge, but simply understanding the differences between property/casualty risks and human asset risks. Let's talk about what I call the *"property/casualty mentality"*. Most property/casualty agents are trained to provide solutions to mitigate the risks associated with required

---

[1] Crossing the Line, The National Underwriter Company, 1997

insurance purchases. We cannot secure a mortgage until we provide proof of insurance. We cannot drive our car without the proper insurance coverage. I cannot open my business without worker's compensation coverage. You get the picture. Many of these transactions are just that, transactional. There is a certain "savoir faire" required to successfully manage a property/casualty agency. Clients come to depend upon the professional advice of their property/casualty agent and many have developed long standing relationships.

The last thing a property/casualty agent wants is for an overly aggressive life salesperson to pressure their client to buy voluntary products. Unfortunately, many property/casualty agents hold the life salesperson in low regard. In fact, they often look at us as the "gorillas in suits."

Over the past 35 years, I have heard all the horror stories of how the life guy either, stole my client, cost me an account, or pressured my longtime client to buy something he didn't need. And, I never had any doubts in my mind that all the stories were absolutely true. That's one of the reasons why I wrote the first cross-marketing book. There are many highly skilled and qualified financial services advisors out there. But, few possess the skills to communicate effectively with property/casualty principals.

Here's why. When a property/casualty agency hires a producer, most will come with their cultivated book of business. If an agency hires a financial services advisor, they may assume that he or she also brings a book of cultivated clients. Quite often, that is not the case. The financial services advisor needs prospects and the property/casualty agency has them. That's where it all starts to unravel. Even if the agency opens up its database or marketing list to the new life person, there is seldom a personal introduction to select accounts or support from the other property/casualty agents in the agency. So, I think you can see how things don't often work when put together in this half-baked approach.

Let's go back to the discussion of risk. Property/casualty risks plus human asset risks equals total risk analysis. Here's what that means. When we approach key accounts of the agency, we should never discuss products, period. In fact, in my first meeting with a commercial client, I will not mention the word "insurance" for several minutes. What I will do is explain exactly what we do as consultants. First, I will explain the property/casualty risks that their agent has covered so well over the years. Then, I explain to the client that there is another risk area. We call these risks "human asset risks". Human asset risks are far greater risks than any property/casualty risks. I proceed to explain why I have made such a bold statement. I tell the business owner that when I speak of human asset risks, I'm speaking about him. He built the business, he makes it function every day and he is its most important asset (most businesses are small Sub S corporations where the owner is actively involved in the success of the firm). He can always rebuild an office or replace a delivery truck, but what if something happens to him? At that point, both the property/casualty producer and the client begin to see just how important it is to address human asset risks. I proceed to tell the client that we do the same thing on the human asset side as his agent did on the property/casualty side. We'll evaluate his human asset risks and tell him what he can do to mitigate some, none, or all of the risks. Our job is merely to act as an agency consultant to make sure he has addressed all the potential risks his business may face.

If the client chooses to proceed at that point, I will inform him that I need another 30-45 minutes to see how he feels about a few things, affording me a chance to more formally present options available to him.

What we have done is present a totally service oriented presentation to the client. Not only does the client understand exactly what we do in the agency, but sincerely appreciates the opportunity to meet with us. The property/casualty principal also understands our approach, as it is really only another form of risk mitigation. Once the agency principal understands total risk analysis, you will be introduced to all the key accounts in the agency. You will never have success in a property/casualty until the principal and the agents trust you. And, now that they know exactly what you do, the sky is the limit.

The entire presentation takes less than three minutes and, as previously mentioned, I never say the word "insurance".

The human asset risk presentation is but a small part of the AgencyMaxx program, although vital to meeting with both personal lines and commercial lines clients.

Introducing AgencyMaxx, a unique turnkey marketing system designed to fill all the gaps not available in other cross-marketing programs. AgencyMaxx consists of multiple modules, designed to assist the property/casualty agency in generating consistent financial services sales without a high level of expertise or excessive time commitment. We can execute successful marketing campaigns on a profitable platform, regardless of the size or mix of business in the agency.

CHAPTER 2

Strategic Window

In the July 1978 issue of the *Journal of Marketing*, Harvard Associate Professor of Business Administration Derek Abell wrote an article that is as timely today as it was some thirty-eight years ago. His article titled "Strategic Windows: The time to Invest in a Product or Market is When a Strategic Window is Open"[2].

Strategic market planning involves the management of any business unit in the dual tasks of anticipating and responding to changes which affect the marketplace for their products. The term "strategic window" is used to focus attention on the fact that there are only limited periods during which the fit between the key requirements of a market and the particular competencies of a firm competing in that market is at an optimum. Investment in a product line or market area should be timed to coincide with periods in which such a strategic window is open.

It's a fact that 25% of independent life agents are over age 60, with the average age of all independent life agents skewing in the late 50's. On the other hand, the need for life insurance is

---

[2] Derek F. Abell, Journal of Marketing 42, no.3 (1978): 21-26

going the other way. Less than half of middle market consumers, ages 25 to 64, have individual life insurance coverage. Forty-four percent of those without life coverage say they need it, and three in ten think they might buy in the next year. Generation Y consumers are the most likely to purchase life insurance.[3]

So you can see that we have, in fact, validated the "Strategic Window" concept, particularly when it comes to supply and demand. We have an increasing marketplace for life insurance sales, while experiencing a decreasing number of independent agents. We also know that the "Millennials" have exceeded the "Boomers" in numbers. So, the available marketplace for life products will continue to increase.

With the facts as they are, the distribution of life products must change. We can no longer count on the diminishing number of independent agents to dominate the marketplace. Logically, the distribution has and will continue to shift to those entities that have the necessary data to prospect for these potential customers.

The four potential candidates are: The banks, the brokerage firms, the property/casualty agencies, and the government. At first, the banks took the simple route, selling fixed annuities and any other easy to market transactional products. The big brokerage firms are now owned by the banks, providing a new level of sophistication and sales opportunities. In addition, all the large wire houses (including those owned by the banks) are serviced by third party distribution companies. By servicing, I'm referring specifically to highly qualified "point of sale" advisors.

---

[3] LIMRA Life Insurance Consumer Studies

One example is Saybrus Partners. Saybrus comes from the Scottish Gaelic word for wealth. Working as an independent distribution company, their priority is not on promoting a given product, but on serving clients' best interests. They can identify the most appropriate products and services, while providing financial professionals the kind of planning expertise and support they need. Their team (average of 15 years of industry experience) is able to provide in depth consultation and strategies for:

Basic insurance protection
Supplemental retirement planning
Legacy building
Tax-efficient cash accumulation and wealth transfer
Asset maximization
Estate preservation and equalization
Strategies for business owners

In just a few years, Saybrus has become the number one third party distribution company in the country. Edward W. Cassidy, Managing Partner, obviously recognized the "strategic window" opening when Saybrus entered the marketplace as the new kid on the block.

To date, few, if any, distribution companies have offered the quality of support for property/casualty agencies just described by Saybrus. Until now. Welcome to AgencyMaxx.

As a property/casualty agency, the "strategic window" of opportunity is now open. I would be begging the question if I asked why you haven't taken advantage of this incredible chance for growth. First of all, until now, many of you did not have any third-party assistance. And, if you did, it may not have worked out. This less than functional relationship may have been caused by several factors, including a weak relationship as well as a poor plan. Unfortunately, it has been the rule, and not the exception to the rule in most cases.

With AgencyMaxx and AgencyLite, we have developed two platforms for property/casualty agencies that are catalysts for proactivity, not reactivity. As you'll discover, AgencyMaxx is designed to work with the agency to develop a total marketing platform, from lead generation to point of sale. All Certified AgencyMaxx Advisors have been vetted and run through a rigorous training regimen, created exclusively for property/ casualty agencies.

AgencyLite, on the other hand, can be implemented in any agency of any size. It's a scaled down version of AgencyMaxx, built for turnkey success. You'll be up and running within a week or two. We'll provide all the tools you'll need to immediately increase your revenues without having to leave your office.

You've got all the necessary data and the relationship with your clients. We'll help you pull it all together without increasing expenses. It's time for your agency to take advantage of the "strategic window" now open!

CHAPTER 3

Getting Started

After defining the need and the potential benefits of cross-marketing financial services, Littell and McSpadden address the tactics for cross-selling life insurance about half way through the book. Assuming the property/casualty agency has not yet become discouraged, they pose one of the most important questions: Where do we start? They go on to summarize the starting requirements: *"P&C shops must expect to do no less: real training, serious coaching, follow-up, monitoring, feedback – all must be provided. Just hanging up a "Life Insurance" shingle will accomplish nothing. Everyone in the shop must be aware of the expansion, and must know enough about the objectives to recognize opportunities as they arise. Additionally, producers must be trained, and regularly "drilled" in the practice of asking more of the right kinds of questions. We suggest that the Sales Manager prepare a series of one-page outlines, containing questions regarding life and benefits needs that are applicable to various types of customers and insist that the questions be asked on sales and service calls"*[4].

---

[4] Crossing the Line, Sales Strategies for Life & Health in the P&C Agency, p91

Here again, although Littell and McSpadden are one hundred percent on target, many property/casualty principals will throw up their arms at this point and tell us they don't have time to do all that is necessary to create the program. What they are really saying is that they do not want to spend the time or money to go through all the steps outlined to succeed. Although they understand the potential profitability and the benefits to the agency, they will not commit.

So, would more agencies commit to a life and annuity cross-marketing platform if a consulting firm built the program for them? Furthermore, the firm is willing to provide the consulting services without charging any fees. They are willing to build and execute the programs for you and are compensated only after they produce results. As a wholesale brokerage and consulting firm, their compensation comes from the insurance companies, not from your profitability.

What I have just described is the AgencyMaxx program. In reality, many agencies will slowly work their way into the total marketing platform, and many will only adopt AgencyLite. Let me go into a bit more detail. We've build the AgencyMaxx program to accommodate almost all agencies, especially doable with the addition of our Certified AgencyMaxx Advisors.

As previously mentioned, all AgencyMaxx Advisors have been vetted relative to their sales and advanced financial services knowledge, but have also been trained in the art of marketing to property/casualty clients. There is a substantial difference between making a sales call to a prospect off the street, and marketing to a commercial lines client. Still, many agencies will move slowly as far as working with a third-party advisor. In that case, we'll probably start with the AgencyLite platform and work our way up to AgencyMaxx. Either way, it's a win-win for the agency.

CHAPTER 4

The Approach

Approaching the property/casualty principal is one of the most difficult parts of the AgencyMaxx program. Here is an example of how we suggest our Advisors approach an agency principal. I have attempted to highlight the important points to discuss to secure the appointment.

There are several roadblocks to overcome when first contacting an agency:

- *Too busy with P/C business to devote any time to financial services*
- *Tried it and failed*
- *Not their area of expertise*
- *Don't trust aggressive life agents*

These are just some of the objections an advisor will encounter when approaching an agency. I suggest the advisor ask the principal for just 30 minutes to share a program that works, and, essentially costs them nothing!

I also suggest the advisor inform the principal that he will only offer this program to a limited number of agencies.

Selectivity and preferential treatment may help him get through the door.

Advisors are aware that all business owners want to increase their profitability in a cost-effective way, and present the AgencyMaxx platform with passion and commitment. Here is an example of the initial telephone approach:

Good morning Mr. Smith. My name is John Jacobs. I work with The Bollinger Companies, an MGA specializing in the cross-marketing of financial services to select property/casualty agencies. You may have seen them interviewed or featured in "Rough Notes" and The National Underwriter.

The purpose of my call is to schedule a brief appointment with you to introduce AgencyMaxx, a guaranteed and unique cross-marketing program created by The Bollinger Companies. I'd like you to know right up front, there are no fees or costs to participating agencies (If principal agrees, schedule the appointment. If asked for more information, continue).

AgencyMaxx is designed to provide a cross-marketing platform for your agency based on service, not product sales. We integrate property/casualty risks with human asset risks in a very professional and totally effective approach. In addition, we can provide a consistent drip marketing campaign generating leads on a regular basis. If you would like to substantially increase your revenues, please allow me 30 minutes of your time to tell you a bit more about AgencyMaxx.

(Schedule the appointment, If the principal still balks, make him two promises:)

1. *Our 30 minutes together will be time well spent, regardless of the outcome, and*

2. *There will not be a second appointment unless you see fit to invite me back. Fair enough?*

If nothing more, we have had the opportunity to meet each other and I'd like to offer you a free copy of Marlin Bollinger's book, "Cross Marketing, Here's Your Wake-Up Call"

The advisor will go over the details of the AgencyMaxx program and offer the principal the opportunity to participate in a personal webinar with me detailing the power of AgencyMaxx.

CHAPTER 5

The Transition

It all started in late 1981 when I was interviewed by the Travelers Life, Health, and Financial Services Department. The key word here is Department. We all know Travelers as a property/casualty company. After spending a decade in the radio and advertising industries, I relocated to Florida and could not find another programming position in the radio industry. So, like so many others, I accepted a position to sell life insurance. In the early 1980's, insurance companies were anxious to hire potential agents and pay a base salary to provide a few years of training.

Although I joined Travelers in 1981, I got into the business in 1978 as an agent for The Equitable and later with State Mutual. When I joined the Travelers in 1981, the position was presented as a Production Supervisor. The role of a Production Supervisor was different from my previous role as a selling agent. With Travelers, I would be making life, annuity, and health sales for property/casualty agents.

I figured out early on with State Mutual that if I became technically astute in concept and product knowledge, I could close sales for less experienced agents and split the case. That experience proved invaluable when joining Travelers. Instead of closing sales for newbies that were on the edge of failing, I could parlay that experience to selling for property/casualty agents.

There was a substantial difference, however, between the presentations I learned as a career agent and the Travelers methodology. The most difficult part of prospecting in the career side was finding qualified prospects. In fact, that's how I figured out that if I had the sales skills and product knowledge, I could let the other agents do the prospecting and I would just go along to make the sale.

If you have ever been on the career side of the life business, you know about the dreaded Monday night calls to secure your ten appointments for the coming week. That was heavy lifting for me, so I found a better way to survive. When joining Travelers, I had the experience necessary to do the job. I was assigned a unit consisting of several locally contracted property/casualty agencies. My role was to accompany the agent on sales calls as the Travelers life expert and close the sale.

Although all life insurance companies use some kind of needs analysis approach, Travelers approach focused on the commercial side of the business. I closed many small sales, however, our goal was to get in front of an agency's larger commercial clients. Neil Rackham[5], author of *"Spin Selling"*, looks at sales in two dimensions: small sales and large sales. Per Mr. Rackham, *"It's about the larger sale. Almost all existing books on selling have used models and methods that were developed in low-value, one-call sales. The traditional strategies of how to sell just don't work in the fast-moving and complex environment of today's major sale. Many of the things that help you in smaller sales will hurt your success*

---

[5] Neil Rackham, *Spin Selling*, (McGraw-Hill, 1988)

as the sale grows larger. Major sales demand a new and different set of skills."

The Travelers presentation was completely different from what I learned at the Equitable or State Mutual. When in front of a commercial client, our goal was not to close a sale on the first call or even to discuss any products. Our goal was simple; explain to the client the difference between property/casualty risks and human asset risks and offer a service called "Total Risk Analysis".

Our presentation consisted of three parts:

1. The Ben Duffy
2. Human Asset Risk Analysis
3. ASP (Appropriate Subsequent Presentation)

The Ben Duffy: Who am I, why am I here, and how do I do business.

Human Asset Risk Analysis: Explains the difference between property/casualty risks and human asset risks.

Appropriate Subsequent Presentation: In the early 1980's most corporations were "C" corporations. The ASP showed how a dollar flows through the corporate structure from top to bottom, focusing on the tax advantaged methods of reducing the final taxable amount.

If the presentation was presented properly, the client completely understood why we were there and more importantly, the potential human asset risks to consider. I learned early on that if I was to successfully market a voluntary product, I first had to disturb the potential client. Let me put that statement in other words: The client should realize by the end of my presentation that there are risks not yet covered that could substantially damage their business.

Following the ASP, I asked the client for a second appointment. I explained that in this appointment I wanted to know how he or she feels about a few things. The Travelers presentation serves to validate Rackham's premise that closing techniques in smaller sales will hurt your success in larger sales. In *"Spin Selling"*, SPIN is a series of questions geared to successfully close the larger sale:

- <u>Situation Questions</u> – *Could you tell me about your company's growth plans?* Although situation questions have an important fact finding role, successful people don't overuse them because too many can bore or irritate the buyer.
- <u>Problem Questions</u> – *Are you concerned about the quality of service provided by your employees?* Problem questions explore problems, difficulties, and dissatisfactions in areas where the seller's product can help. Inexperienced people generally don't ask enough problem questions.
- <u>Implication Questions</u> – *How will this problem affect your future profitability?* Implication questions take a customer problem and explore its effects or consequences. By asking these questions, successful people help the customer understand a problem's seriousness or urgency. Implication questions are particularly important in large sales, and even very experienced salespeople rarely ask them well.
- <u>Need-payoff Questions</u> – *If we could improve the quality of this operation, how would that help you?* Need-payoff

questions should get the customer to tell you the benefits that your solution could offer.

The Travelers presentation focused heavily on two of Rackham's SPIN stages: Implication and Need-payoff questions. For example, an implication question would be.... *What would happen to your business if you were suddenly taken out of the picture?* An example of a needs-payoff question would be.... *Would you sleep better tonight if you knew I was working on some solutions to eliminate your human asset risks?*

The large sale is not a one call close and requires a greater skillset than the simpler sale.

Quite often, the property/casualty agent will look at the life agent as a "gorilla in a suit", just one step above a used car salesman. Right or wrong, we are often perceived as being overly aggressive, utilizing one call closing techniques. As salespeople, we've all heard or been exposed to the old standard closes:

Assumptive -When would you like to schedule the exam?

Alternative – Would you like the $500,000 or the $1,000,000 policy?

Last-chance – I hear the rates will be going up next week, so unless....

Order-blank – Filling out the application even though the buyer has not indicated a willingness to make a buying decision.

Rackham discovered a few more quick closes, many of which are new to me also: The Sharp Angle, Ben Franklin, Puppy Dog, Colombo, Double-reverse Whammo, Banana, and Half-Open.

Rackham goes on to state that *"No other area of selling skill is as popular as closing. This is true however you measure it, whether by number of words written, number of instructional hours, or number of feet of training films endured by each new generation of salespeople."*

AgencyMaxx and AgencyLite consist of a series of modules designed to work with any agency of any size or mix of business. Although the large sale may be favored over the small sale, that does not mean that we should not grant credence to any modular programs that provide the opportunity for consistent sales, regardless of size. The important thing is to get started by developing some form of financial services cross-marketing.

A few years ago, McKinsey & Company released a whitepaper entitled: *"Agents of the Future: The Evolution of Property and Casualty Insurance Distribution".* [6] The whitepaper created quite a stir among independent agencies because of what many believed to be a gloom and doom view of the independent distribution system. Here's how it started: *"Local agents have long been an integral part of the property and casualty insurance landscape, and continue to serve an important role as advisors and intermediaries. However, there has been a gradual shift in the value that carriers and customers place on many activities traditionally performed by local agents, which is increasingly calling into question what role they will play in the future.*

Where agents once served as the front line in risk selection and pricing, advances in predictive models are making this role obsolete. Perhaps the most disruptive to the traditional agent value

---

[6] McKinsey & Company, Agents of the Future, 2012

model, auto insurance – which accounts for 70 percent of personal lines premiums – is fast becoming commoditized."

The McKinsey report also highlighted some bright spots for those agencies that evolve into multi-channel marketing and offer a stronger value proposition. In fact, McKinsey noted that *"those agencies that can adapt to a new set of circumstances will thrive."* The report identifies travel agents as facing similar dis-intermediating forces. Although many of these agencies have gone by the wayside, others have survived by reinventing their business models, focusing on more complex travel and specialization.

I'd be preaching to the choir if I brought up flat commissions, lack of contingencies, and increased operating costs. In the future, it will be absolutely imperative to be able to do more with less.

In Broker Central's blog, author Paul Shott writes: *"Auto insurance, once the bread and butter of the P&C agency, has devolved to the line of business with the thinnest margin. To sum it up, P&C agencies face downward pressure on premium and revenue growth while at the same time juggling increased costs for agency management systems, technology improvements, and website updates. Agency principals need strategies to increase revenue and profitability without adding equivalent expenses. Only one strategy accomplishes all three objectives and improves customer satisfaction at the same time: cross-selling."*

McKinsey goes on to state that the number of P&C agents has declined by 10 percent between 1995 and 2011. [7] Contrary to McKinsey's stated decline, the IIABA's Agency Universe

---

[7] Source: A.M. Best 10K reports; IIABA Phocus Wright: ARC; ASTA.org

Study found that the number of independent agencies has actually grown from 37,500 to 38,500 from 2010-2012, for the first time in several years.[8] Jeff Yates of the IIABA" *believes the continuing strength of the agency force results from two factors that McKinsey does not even acknowledge in its report: (1) the continuing importance of personal relationships in insurance (agents have them, most carriers don't) and (2) the greater trust many consumers have in individuals they personally know and do business with, as compared to large institutions".*

No doubt, Mr. Yates got it right. AgencyMaxx and AgencyLite are built on a foundation of agent/client relationships. Both programs have been designed to perpetuate the strong relationship between the agency and the client, while paying close attention to cost efficiencies.

Dave Goodwin[9], a former P/C agency principal and an insurance cross-selling consultant, summarizes the most powerful reason for cross-selling in just two sentences: *"Cross-selling remains virtually untouched, with a potential limited only by your creativity. Ignoring it means inviting competitors to sell to – and eventually own – your client base."* Goodwin has an uncanny ability to lay it out in very clear terms: *"Today's property/casualty agency is no longer in just the P/C business: It's a segment of the financial services industry. Insurance is no longer a free-standing product or service, but part of a professional package. CPA's are selling insurance, as are stockbrokers, publishers, department stores, gas companies, and or course, banks. However, these new distribution sources still lack a key characteristic that defines you as an independent agent: the ability to develop your cross-selling*

---

[8] Yates, Jeff, IIABA, 2013
[9] Goodwin, Dave, Complete Markets, 2013

potential. No online vendor or non-agency that markets insurance can cross sell its clients as effectively as you can."

There is no doubt that cross-marketing financial services is the most cost effective way to solidify your book, increase your bottom line, and most importantly, provide a great service to the clients that mean so much to you and your agency.

CHAPTER 6

Reactivity

I hope I have convinced you by now that cross- marketing financial services is the direction you want to take your agency or your book of business, if an agent. What I haven't shared with you in much detail, is how to make it happen. Many of you want to take the next step but do not know how. Over the past 35 years, the agencies I have consulted have been less than aggressively proactive. What that means in plain English is that you have a life insurance license, you keep up with your CE, but you do not promote life and annuity products, either overtly or covertly through a few paragraphs of general jargon on your website. Remember what Littell and McSpadden said earlier: *"Just hanging up a "Life Insurance" shingle will accomplish nothing."*

As I mentioned in the Preface of this publication, there is little research available about cross-marketing, let alone an in depth how to guide. Of course, Littell and McSpadden did write a how to guide in *"Crossing the Line"* but, in my opinion, they went too far.

Here's what I mean. They covered almost every base and, if an agency qualifies as big enough with the funds to start a cross-marketing program from scratch, then *"Crossing the Line"* has great value. To many others, they offer too much too soon.

I recently met with a marketing executive from the FAIA (Florida Association of Independent Agents). The purpose of my visit was to share with the Association the details of the AgencyMaxx program and its benefit to the members of the Association. There is no doubt that our discussion was beneficial to both of us. I discussed the need for turnkey marketing assistance in the agencies. He then informed me that many Association member agencies are under one million in premium. He complimented us on our successes with some of the largest agencies in the state and questioned our value to the smaller agencies. His comment was truly thought provoking.

Thought provoking in that he assumed we would not be interested in working with the smaller agencies or perhaps a relationship with smaller agencies would not be profitable. Both assumptions are incorrect. We welcome the opportunity to work with smaller agencies. In many instances, they need our help more than larger agencies.

As Littell and McSpadden so eloquently lay out all the steps necessary to create a viable cross-selling program, it's just not viable for smaller agencies. That's why we created AgencyLite.

Rackham's distinction between small sales and large sales is correct. The differences between these closing approaches will become more evident as we discuss the AgencyMaxx Data Management program in more detail. Do not assume that small agencies will only be involved with small sales. We assume the bulk of their sales will be smaller than larger agencies, but even smaller agencies have a few clients that can generate big tickets.

Both large and small agencies have fallen into the web of reactivity. Deloitte Research[10] conducted a pair of surveys of 1,071 consumers with life insurance coverage and 1,000 without life insurance coverage. The surveys focused on three distinct perspectives: How respondents think about life insurance, a look at their past purchase experiences, as well as a peek ahead into how (and how much) respondents intend to buy in the near term. While life insurance is not the top priority for most, the coverage is very prominent on the to-do list for many respondents. The survey found that a significant number of consumers intend to buy a new policy in the next two years, both among those currently without insurance as well as among respondents looking for additional coverage beyond what they already have.

The survey revealed a fundamental failure to communicate, as many of those who are currently uninsured noted that a prime reason they don't have coverage is no one has asked them to buy it. Even those with insurance open to buying additional coverage often say they have not received offers from their agents or carriers. Carriers and agencies cannot wait for prospects to seek them out, as many respondents said they don't shop for life insurance on their own initiative.

Life insurance, in almost all instances, is a voluntary buy, whereas, almost all property/casualty products are a mandatory buy. So, providing a little blurb on your website about life insurance, just ain't gonna do it. Any life insurance you do sell is almost always the result of reactivity.

Here are two great examples of reactivity. Ask yourself if either of these scenarios have ever happened to you.

---

[10] Can P&C Agents Boost Income with Life Insurance Sales, Property Casualty 360, July 2012

- Long standing client #1 tells you that he just bought $2 million of life insurance from the Northwestern agent down the block. Surprised, you tell the client that you have a life insurance license and you could have sold him the coverage. At that point, the client says...." ***You never told me".***

- Long standing client #2 approaches you and tells you that his accountant (no life license) wants you to buy $2 million of life insurance to cover the key person needs of his company. Obviously, this is a more favorable scenario than the situation with client #1. You are happy that the client asked you to fulfill his request and immediately approach one of the BGA's that has been emailing you, to request a quote. Instead of inquiring further or bringing in the cavalry, you offer the lowest premium on a ten-year term contract, assuming that all term life insurance is the same, and also that price is the driving factor.

You cannot expect to be an expert on life insurance coverages, even though term insurance is the simplest coverage to understand. What you may not know is that term insurance contracts can differ significantly, particularly when it comes to conversion options. In addition, another form of life insurance may provide more flexibility and greater options for the client and his business. We'll discuss bringing in the cavalry when we explain the role of the Certified AgencyMaxx Advisor.

As you can see from the two examples and the Deloitte surveys, reactivity will not produce measurable results.

CHAPTER 7

Proactivity

The most difficult thing, from a consultant's point of view, is generating proactivity in the property/casualty agency. Whenever I speak to a group of agency principals and explain *Total Risk Analysis,* their response is always positive. If I can get twenty agency decision makers in a room, at least fifteen of them will be ready to move forward after the meeting. That's where the frustration sets in and the real work begins.

Although the principals have great intentions, other priorities in the agencies somehow seem to hijack our cross-marketing initiatives. Over the years, I've learned to take one step at a time, easing my way into many agencies.

Brian Leising[11] of Financial Brokerage wrote an interesting article on *"Three Ways for a Property Casualty Agency to Sell More Life Insurance". "Selling auto and homeowners insurance involves sales skills, but selling life insurance requires a different skill set, a different approach. People are not required to purchase life insurance. The lowest price is not going to make the sale. You have to make them realize they need the coverage. You cannot*

---

[11] Leising, Brian, Financial Brokerage, Inc., February 2015

throw out numbers of different coverage amounts and expect them to pick one. You need a system in place to determine the amount and type of coverage needed for your client's situation".

Here again, it's like Déjà vu all over again.... selling life insurance isn't the same as selling property/casualty insurance and you cannot have a successful cross-marketing program without a plan.

Tim Gilder[12], CLU, ALMI, wrote an article on cross-selling in the 2014 PIA National Agency Marketing Guide. *"Cross-selling life insurance to your current customers is a great idea. In fact, it is such a great idea that I bet you have been told to do it at least fifty times in the past five years. So? Go do it! What's stopping you? Tell every single one of your agents and CSR's that the next time they are on the phone with someone all they have to say is "Do you need any life insurance?" and money will start falling from the sky. That is all there is to cross-selling life insurance. Right?*

Obviously, it is not that easy. In fact, I would argue that successfully cross-selling life insurance is extremely difficult. Unless you get some help you will be disappointed with the results and will not look to do it very often".

Cross-selling life insurance is difficult, and you certainly need a plan. You must understand the difference between reactivity and proactivity. And, you do need hand holding help through the entire process!

You can see why Gilder so openly acknowledges the frustrations that so many agencies have experienced. Moving from a position of reactivity to one of proactivity requires a total

---

[12] Gilder, Tom, "Building a Cross-selling Machine", PIA National Agency Marketing Guide, 2014

consulting effort that most BGA's are not equipped to handle. We all know how to *"talk the talk"* but few of us can *"walk the walk."*

In 2015, Barry Seigerman[13]wrote an article for Property Casualty 360 asking why P/C agents are not selling life and health products. He identified six excuses and the reality debunking them. Mr. Seigerman starts off by identifying two of the biggest sales ever made in his agency. *"Two of the biggest sales we ever made amounted to total premiums of $1.4 million and $1.8 million, and originated with a small, local, personal lines customer generating annual commissions of about $400. The customer had become the president of one of the largest independent beverage distributor associations and invited us to submit a proposal. We made the sale. The next year we were referred to another association, and were again successful. Both customers remained with us for several years until the associations were disbanded. Consider this: $3.2 million of new premium, from one small personal lines customer!"*

When speaking with a newly recruited property/casualty agency, I often share one of our own success stories. We met with a second-generation agency principal several times to discuss the value of cross-marketing. He understood the value but was slow to commit to an agency backed platform. During the discussions, we helped him identify a few prospects that had a strong and loyal relationship with the agency. Shortly thereafter, one of my Sales Vice Presidents received a call asking if we could review one of the agency's commercial accounts life insurance policies.

Keep in mind that the agent was licensed, but had absolutely no idea how to review the existing policies. That's where we came

[13] Seigerman, Barry, "Why aren't you cross-selling Life and Health products? 6 excuses and the reality", Property Casualty 360, august, 2015

in. We analyzed all existing coverages, made recommendations, and helped the agent earn a commission of $300,000.

A few weeks later, we were contacted by another property/casualty agent. One of his long-time clients had been recently widowed and had just purchased a $1 million, single premium permanent life policy from another agent. Having second thoughts, she asked the property/casualty agent to review the issued policy. Here again, the agent scanned and emailed the contract to us for review. We immediately realized the issued policy had only thirteen days remaining in the free look period. Bottom line, in less than thirteen days we were able to secure a solid offer from a more competitive company. By doing so, we saved the client over $13,000, and paid the agent a $20,000 commission.

Both examples demonstrate the relationship the agents had with their clients. When I was making joint sales calls with a property/casualty agent, the client would not sign the application without consulting the agent. If the agent gave a positive nod, the client signed.

Let's go back to the six excuses identified by Mr. Seigerman:

Concern – *"I'm too busy handling my customers, staff, carriers, etc., to have the time to learn and become licensed in all the different areas."*

Reality – *"Commit to delegating most of those tasks on which you spend an excessive amount of time. **However, what should never be delegated is your responsibility as a leader to create a business vision and establish a mission.**"*

His last sentence is so important in making a cross-marketing program a success. The AgencyMaxx platform is not fee based, but does require a strong commitment from the participating agency regarding vision and mission.

Concern – *"I can't have expertise in every insurance or financial product of service."*

Reality – *"True, but you can become licensed and add staff who have special skills and expertise so that the customer's needs are met by the organization, not by a single individual. For example, I've sold a ton of different policies over my many years in the business, but I haven't rated a single policy myself since I obtained my P&C license in the 60's. Does the chairman of general Motors have to know how to do a brake job?"*

As we go into more detail about the AgencyMaxx platform, you will realize the extent of the services we are capable of providing. In most situations, there is no need to add staff. If you do not have the internal expertise to handle the call, we will happily introduce you to one on our Certified AgencyMaxx Advisors.

Concern – *"We have to focus on building our P&C book of business to be profitable, grow and satisfy our agency companies. There aren't enough commissions in Life and Annuity to make it worthwhile"*

Reality – *"Building an insurance agency with a balanced book of business that generates revenues from diversified sources leads to more rapid and predictable growth and serves the agency well* *during the underwriting cycles and economic ups and downs. It also gives you the chance to base your annual planning on those areas that offer the best profit results."*

Concern – *"We can't make money on small commercial accounts. We need to focus only on commercial P&C accounts that generate large premiums."*

Reality – *Yes, you can make money on small commercial accounts if you establish a minimum revenue threshold and cross-sell personal and Life products."*

Concern – *We can't make money in personal P&C lines of business," or "Our producers won't sell personal lines."*

Reality – *Yes, you can. You will likely find that some of the commercial customers with the largest commissions came from some of the smallest personal lines customers who own businesses or who have many business relationships. It's important to establish revenue thresholds for personal lines."*

Concern – *"I don't have the money to hire and finance producers for each specific area, nor the staff to support them and to service the customer."*

Reality – *"Producers and staff should be encouraged to learn to sell and service multi-lines. True, it takes time and commitment to hire and train the best people you can find, but it will pay off. If you have a good business plan and show that you are growing, it's a lot easier to borrow money from traditional lending sources. You can* *also partner with other professionals like registered investment advisors, and outside brokers."*

Keep all these concerns in your mind as we discuss the AgencyMaxx platform. You will notice that we address each concern identified by Mr. Seigerman, and provide a practical solution.

CHAPTER 8

AgencyMaxx

Introducing AgencyMaxx, the first total marketing maximization turn-key system, built exclusively for property/casualty agencies. AgencyMaxx brings all the essential elements of a P/C cross-marketing program together:

- Data management
- Lead generation
- Total risk analysis
- A powerful suite of selling tools
- Agency contact management
- In house quoting and application tools
- Professional backroom consultants
- Step by step sales process
- Certified point of sale AgencyMaxx advisors

Would you sell more life insurance and annuities if...

- All leads were provided for you
- You had a simple in house multi carrier quoting and selling tool

- You had professional backup point of sale help for the difficult cases
- You worked directly with one of the country's top P/C marketing firms
- You could increase your bottom line without increasing your expenses
- You improved client retention

Isn't it time to MAXXimize your marketing?

I have shared with you the language from our most recent *"Rough Notes"* ad.

AgencyMaxx and AgencyLite evolved from a presentation utilized by Travelers back in my Production Supervisor days. When I first packaged the presentation, I named it the *"Travelers Alliance Program"*. The presentation was, and is geared to commercial accounts. As mentioned previously, part of the Program consists of a discussion about *"Total Risk Analysis"*. The presentation is carefully crafted to explain to the client the difference between property/casualty risks and human asset risks. We emphasize the fact that human asset risks are substantially greater than any property/casualty risk the client will ever face. Here again, we intentionally do not mention the word *"insurance"* in the presentation. Remember, my role was to act as a consulting representative of the agency, and not as a life salesman.

When working with commercial accounts, we are categorizing them in Rackham's large sale group. Although the larger sale is important, we cannot ignore creating marketing programs geared to the smaller sale. That's where *"The Alliance Program"* fell short. As we go further into the MarketMaxx system, I'll explain how we create smaller sales, utilizing a presentation for personal lines clients as well as turn-key quoting tools and target marketing.

The entire *"Human Asset Risk Analysis"* (HARA) for commercial clients should not take more than three minutes. In that short time, your client will thoroughly understand just how important your presentation can be to his family and his business. Here is the presentation:

Remember, our initial presentation starts off with *"The Ben Duffy"*:

- Who am I?
- Why am I here?
- How do I do business?

Ben Duffy grew up in Hells Kitchen in New York. He started working in the mailroom at BBD&O, an advertising agency. Ben worked his way from the mailroom all the way up to the presidency of the agency. As President, he was on his way to make a presentation to the President of the American Tobacco Company. On his way to the appointment, Mr. Duffy thought of three questions he may be asked during the appointment. Thus, the beginning of *"The Ben Duffy"*.

Commercial Risk Analysis Presentation

"In response to that **"How do I do business?"** *question, Mr./ Ms. Client, let me say that a significant part of my job is to provide clients of the _____ agency with an important service called* **"Human Asset Risk Analysis"**.

Let me explain specifically what that is. All individuals are exposed to risks of almost every description, but those risks really break down into two categories: **Property Risks and Human Asset Risks.**

In your dealings with _____, I know he/she has carefully explained the property risks you face every day....fire, water damage, work interruption, and all the other things that can endanger your business and its operation.

In each case, you had a decision to make:

- *To cover **ALL** of the risk*
- *To cover **PART** of the risk*
- *To cover **NONE** of the risk*

In determining this, you and _____ worked as a team, and once the risks were analyzed and all the facts were weighed, he/she helped you select the best course of action for you to take in the light of your individual situation.

It is also important to follow that very same risk analysis procedure in another risk area...the human asset side of your business, because that represents an even greater risk to your business than any potential damage to your business.

Now, when I speak of the **"Human Asset Risks",** *Mr./Ms. Client, I'm primarily talking about* **YOU.** *You built this business, you manage it, and you make it run. Without you, it will undergo drastic change, and may even cease to exist. Because human beings are mortal, it is a certainty that it must someday operate without you. When that day comes Mr./Ms. Client, certain things will happen to your business...all of them bad. We feel it is important for these risks to be analyzed and explained to eliminate them.*

When we do that, you will have the same decisions to make as you had on the property side:

- *To cover **ALL** of the risk*
- *To cover **PART** of the risk*
- *To cover **NONE** of the risk*

These decisions are entirely yours to make. Our job is to point out the risks, explain what they are, and give you our recommendations on what can be done to reduce or eliminate them. Fair enough?"

If presented properly, this presentation will be the most important three minutes you spend with any commercial account!

The old Travelers presentation did not provide a comparable presentation for the personal lines client. As demonstrated, don't always look at the personal lines client as a small sale. Remember, Barry Seigerman turned a $400 commission into a $1.8 million payday.

Personal Lines Risk Analysis Presentation

*"In response to that **"How do I do business?"** question, Mr./ Ms. Client, let me say that a significant part of my job is to provide clients of the _____ agency with an important service called* **"Human Asset Risk Analysis".**

Let me explain specifically what that is. All individuals are exposed to risks of almost every description, but those risks really *break down into two categories:* **Property Risks and Human Asset Risks.**

In the past, we focused on the property risks you face, and offered solutions to eliminate or reduce those risks. An example of those risks would be insuring your autos, home, and any liability exposures you may face.

It is also important to follow that very same risk analysis procedure in another risk area, the **Human Asset Risks** you face every day. **Human Asset Risks** are risks far greater than any personal property risks you will ever face. When I speak of **Human Asset Risks**, I am talking specifically about **You and your family!**

Because auto and most homeowner's insurance is mandatory, we purchase these coverages. But, unfortunately, when it comes to protecting the things we cherish most, many families fall far short of insuring all the human things that can happen to them during their lifetimes.

We all know someone that has suffered a family tragedy, either through premature death or disability. What would happen to your family if you or your spouse were tragically taken out of the picture tomorrow?

My role is simple; to work with you to ascertain what is most important to you and your family. Then, as a consultant, I will make some suggestions as to what can be done to eliminate or reduce your **Human Asset Risks.**

At that time, you'll have a decision to make:

- To cover **ALL** of the risk
- To cover **PART** of the risk
- To cover **NONE** of the risk

These decisions are entirely yours to make. My job is to point out the risks, explain what they are, and give my recommendations on what should be done about them. Fair enough?

There you have it. We have addressed all the **Human Asset Risks** faced by the commercial, as well as the personal lines client. In both cases, the next step is to schedule a second appointment (fact finding). When asking for the follow-up appointment, I do not refer to it as such, but just tell the client that I would like to meet with them again to see how they feel about a few things.

In our explanation of the **Data Management** segment of the AgencyMaxx program, we'll provide an explanation of our filtering techniques used with both commercial and personal lines clients.

Although smaller accounts can definitely lead to larger sales, we agree with Rackham as far as marketing to, and closing small and large sales. Here again, we'll demonstrate these differences as we delve further into the AgencyMaxx and AgencyLite programs.

CHAPTER 9

Readiness Assessment

Prior to contracting an agency to participate in the AgencyMaxx program, we conduct a *"Readiness Assessment Survey."* The survey is designed to take a cursory look at the agency to determine its' mix of business, volume per line, number of clients, demographics, specialty areas, staff analysis, and their current or previous marketing endeavors.

We want to learn as much about the agency as possible without creating a laundry list of requirements that would discourage an agency from participating.

Most agencies offer both personal and commercial lines, and many have a benefits department. Agencies with a benefits department skew on the commercial side of the business since offering benefits fits very nicely with commercial lines. We have noticed, however, that most benefits sales specialists do not have a very strong understanding of the human asset risks faced by company principals, key personnel, and rank and file employees.

With that in mind, you can readily see the marketing opportunities we can create for individual financial services sales with their commercial and benefits clientele. Identifying this niche when conducting our survey helps us decide how to filter the marketing list.

There are many other examples that will help us create effective filtering when we analyze an accurate survey.

Once our *"Readiness Assessment Survey"* is complete and analyzed, we are ready to move on to step two, building the *"Business Plan."*

CHAPTER 10

Business Plan

Do you remember my comments about Littell and McSpadden in the Getting Started chapter? It is my opinion that the prerequisites they set forth just to get started in cross-marketing were so involved that most agency principals would throw up their arms and move on.

There are, however, steps that must be taken to make the program successful. Building a solid *"Business Plan"* is one of them. Here's why. Every time I interview an agency principal that has tried cross-marketing and failed, I see a common thread. None of these agencies had a plan. Most brought in a life guy the same way they hire property/casualty producers. Well, maybe not exactly the same way, but they certainly do not have a thorough understanding of the role of the life guy and how he can help grow agency revenues.

I've seen the same scenario play out so many times: *"Here's your desk. I'll introduce you to our sales staff and CSR's and ...... good luck. If you need anything, let me know".* The life guy might as well be prospecting from the phone book. Yes, he will get a piece of totally reactive low hanging fruit on occasion, but the deal is ultimately doomed to fail. Why? Simply because it was not build on a plan.

Contrary to all the heavy lifting Littell and McSpadden require of the agency principal, AgencyMaxx will build the business plan based upon our experience and your input. Let us do all the lifting.

CHAPTER 11

Data Management

The most unique proposition of the AgencyMaxx program is that it brings all the essential elements of a property/casualty marketing program together. Getting on the road to proactivity starts with a strong lead generation system.

The first thing we do is work with the agency to understand their CRM. Then we discuss the filters necessary to successfully market to three segments of their clientele:

- Mono-line customers (single auto or homeowners)
- Multi-line clients (auto and homeowners)
- Commercial clients and high net worth

Identifying just three marketing categories is a bit simplistic, since we dissect each category a bit further, particularly the auto and homeowners. You'll notice that I referred to the mono-line folks as customers and the multi-line and commercial accounts as clients. Here again, the more lines a person has with your agency, the less likely they are to shop their account. Mono-line customers shop. You need to make them clients.

Once our marketing department has a handle on the agency's CRM, we work with the agency to create a marketing list, based upon the filtering system described above. Once that is complete, we upload the marketing list. We've driven our first mile on the road to proactivity.

Not all agencies are created equal and it is not uncommon to work with an agency that could use some help with the consolidation of data, bringing it up to date, and applying it to the AgencyMaxx system. If that is the case, we work with the agency to create a suitable marketing list to upload.

By now, you probably have a few questions regarding the criteria used to design the marketing list and the security of your agenda data. We only upload data that is necessary to create effective filtering for each of the three categories. For example, we do not upload social security numbers, corporate tax ID's, or other confidential data. Furthermore, we provide a *"Confidentiality and Security Agreement"*. And, we only contract with established and reputable online collaborative resources.

Arthur Middleton Hughes[14], Vice President of the Data Marketing Institute, has consulted multiple property/casualty companies regarding increasing customer retention. He notes two programs which reduced customer attrition:

- Sell a second policy to existing customers
- Communicate often with customers

Studies have shown that $1 paid towards customer retention increases profits by more than $5 spent on new customer

---

[14] Hughes, Arthur, "Strategic Database Marketing", 3rd ed., McGraw Hill, 2006

acquisition. Hughes goes on to note that *"home and automobile insurance is a tough business. Because of vigorous competition and high acquisition costs, it takes several years before an automobile insurance customer can become profitable. If the customer leaves a year of two after being acquired the insurance company loses money. Travelers knew this but was not able to do much about it. Travelers works through thousands of independent agents who handle insurance for many different companies. A database analyst from CDC set up a communications system for Travelers that worked. From previous experience the analyst knew that:*

- *Similar programs attempted at Travelers had not been successful, however,*
- *Customers want communications. They like to hear from their insurance agents.*
- *To be effective, the communication should come from a local agent, not from national headquarters.*

To begin, it was necessary to sell the program to the independent agents. It met a lot of resistance. They were not convinced:

- *That a retention program was valuable to them*
- *That direct mail would work*
- *That communications could affect when or whether a customer will defect*
- *That the program would have an adequate ROI*
- *That Travelers knew anything about their customers that they didn't already know*

What was finally developed was a retention program, built from a customer database that provided a systematic program delivering high quality communications at a very low cost. The messages were from a local agent. The program provided the agents with a turnkey operation which was simple to buy into, and required almost no work on the part of the agents.

The program developed five annual "touches" which varied with the type of insurance that the customer had, and the length of time that the customer had been with Travelers. The five were:

- *Within 60 days of renewal – An annual review of the policy*
- *Within the 1st quarter – A thank you card*
- *Within the 2nd quarter – A cross-sell postcard*
- *Within the 3rd quarter – A newsletter*
- *Within the 4th quarter – A seasonal greeting card*

The program developers learned that for each customer, they had to determine the appropriate message, the frequency of messages that the customer wanted, the desired channel, the timing of the message, and the likelihood of defection. Statistics showed that 65% of the customers who defected, never talked to an agent before they left. But 80% of the customers who talked to an agent during the year did not leave.

What do customers want from their independent agents? A Customer Retention Survey for Personal Lines Customers conducted by the Independent Insurance Association showed that:

- *52% of insurance customers describe themselves as relationship buyers*
- *The customers want an annual review of the coverage of their policy*

- *They are looking for an agent with integrity who has a stable business*
- *They want information about their policies and coverage*

The program was based upon detailed analysis of the customer database. The program used database data and modeling to determine who was staying and who was leaving. The analysts determined customer profitability and lifetime value. These were used to drive the segmentation and retention strategy. Overall, the program came up with a measurement of customer desirability. Now that the software showed who Travelers wanted to keep, and what they were worth, it was possible to develop and execute a program to modify customer behavior through communications.

So, what did the program accomplish? To measure the success, Travelers compared the retention rates of participants and non-participants. For auto insurance customers, the program was able to increase the retention by 5%. For property insurance, the increase was 4%,

Why did this program succeed whereas the others had failed?

- *The program was not centrally subsidized*
- *In prior programs, the agent risked nothing*
- *In this program, the agent was risking his own money. He wanted it to succeed".*

Having spent 20 years of my insurance career at Travelers, I can certainly confirm the fact that their marketing department experimented many times with various cross-selling programs. Prior to spinning off Travelers Life and Annuity, the parent Company invested in multiple cross- selling programs, not only to cross-market property/casualty products, but also to ingrain into its independent agency force the value of cross-selling financial services. Every failure was a step closer to success. In my 20 years with the Company, we had many failures, but because of all those attempts, we developed a successful financial services model that worked.

Just months before the spinoff, I was asked to assist the home office marketing department in developing their most comprehensive financial services cross-selling initiative to date. The program was called *"Centersource"*, a center for the marketing of financial services within a property casualty agency. There are still some elements of the never to be released *"Centersource"* program being utilized by AgencyMaxx. The program was never released to the independent agency force because Travelers Life and Annuity was spun off as a stand-alone entity prior to the completion of the program.

Hughes made an interesting observation about Travelers when he said that other programs they tried had failed. That comment brought back a memory of my experience as a field vice president working with the home office marketing team. Early on, they told me that the *"Centersource"* program was essentially designed to be a pilot program and not to worry if it didn't work. Honestly, that initial thought process bothered me.

As a Regional Vice President, I was judged by the production generated by my Region. Piloting a program that didn't work would be a waste of my time and the productivity of my Region. I certainly didn't want to dedicate my time to a program that didn't achieve its intended results. That's exactly why Hughes thinks the Travelers program he described worked, the agents had skin in the game. Since my income was directly tied to the production of my region, I also had skin in the game when it came to the success of *"Centersource"*.

To be fair to the home office marketing team, it is my opinion that *"Centersource"* would have been successful. In fact, there are parts of the program being utilized by AgencyMaxx. I think the program would have ultimately been simplified as it had, in my opinion, too many moving parts, representing the quintessential fingerprint of a home office marketing team that was not completely in touch with the realities of where *"the rubber meets the road."*

CHAPTER 12

Filtering

Once we conclude the agreements and upload the agency's marketing list, it is time to determine how we are going to filter the data to achieve the most profitable results. Although all agencies are different, we presented three categorical filters:

- Mono-line customers (single auto or homeowners)
- Multi-line clients (auto and homeowners)
- Commercial clients and high net worth

Although Hughes credited the success of the Travelers program to having skin in the game, he also touched upon the importance of filtering. *"The program developers learned that for each customer, they had to determine the appropriate message, the frequency of messages that the customer wanted, the desired channel, the timing of the message, and the likelihood of defection".*

With customized modifications built into every agency's plan, we initially build the filters as follows:

- Mono-line customers – product offerings
- Multi-line clients – combination of product and concept marketing
- Commercial clients and high net worth – concept marketing

It is fair to say that creating only three filtering categories is somewhat rudimentary, which it is, but we must have a starting point. Once we have established the clients that fall into each category, we look for ideocratic reasons to create necessary sub-filters.

Our logic is that many mono-line customers are, in general, younger people insuring an auto, or possibly a new home, and are possibly most suited to make transactional purchases. That is not to say that these customers may not fall into one of the other categories. Thus, the sub-filtering.

Multi-line clients can be transactional buyers or concept buyers. Either one, we cover all bases by providing a mix of product offerings and timely concepts. An example of promoting a timely concept would be providing information about IRA's between January 1st and April 15th. We would also provide appropriate product information to fund the IRA.

Although commercial accounts and high net worth clients may benefit from some of the same information provided to the multi-line group, they have more specific financial needs and are subjected to additional financial risks. Commercial clients must think about ways to perpetuate their business and the cost of replacing a key employee. High net worth clients are concerned about preserving and passing on their assets to their heirs, while keeping taxes to a minimum.

Marlin Bollinger

Insurance products can provide a solution to many of these potential problems. But before we present product solutions, it is important to educate and remind these commercial and high net worth clients of the potential financial situations they may encounter.

CHAPTER 13

Lead Generation

Once we have uploaded the agency's marketing list, we develop a systematic schedule of email messages based upon our filtering. Our initial email will be sent to customers and clients in all three categories.

The first email, presented in letter form from the agency principal, is a synopsis of the agency's history in the community and their commitment to offer the highest quality of personal service and professionalism. The email goes on to identify the ever-changing financial marketplace and the need to remain contemporary in their marketing of property/casualty and other financial services.

The email announces the establishment of a *"Center of Financial Services"*, positioning the agency to help their clients analyze their personal and business financial needs and goals, including services in the life and annuity areas.

In 1985, I resigned my position at Travelers and established a financial services corporation in a property/casualty agency. Having spent four years as a red-carpet salesman, I had to get out there and do it myself. The agency's core markets were Travelers, Aetna, and the Hartford.

Each of these companies offered their own version of a CSR (customer service representative) generated term selling program. None of these programs worked. Why? Because CSR's are not sales oriented. They are service providers and do not feel comfortable promoting products. With that being said, there are ways for CSR's to play a vital role in promoting the agency's increased presence in life and annuity cross-marketing, without feeling that they are being asked to sell a product.

CSR's are speaking with clients all day long. I do not advocate having them ask for life or annuity sales, but I do suggest that they send the client the introductory email immediately after their conversation. This is a great way to kick start your financial services awareness.

I remained with the agency from 1985-1987. I sold the financial services corporation in April of 1987 and returned to Travelers. Much of what I suggest in this book has been tried and proven successful. Our financial services marketing efforts were successful during the two-year run. I sold the company, having been offered another position with Travelers in their Washington, D.C. office. I was hired to consult and grow the life business in their property/casualty agencies, as I had done in South Florida.

Remember the scenario where the commercial client informs the salesman that he just bought life insurance from another agent. The agent replies that *"I have a life license and could have sold life insurance to you".* The client replies: *"You never told me".* It is vitally important that we inform all agency clients of exactly what we offer, including financial services.

Now that the agency has completed step one in proactivity by sending the introductory email letter and having the CSR's augment the campaign, we're ready to move forward with our planned three category email campaigns.

We've all seen the commercials on television for Select Quote or Matrix Direct, offering term life insurance at the most competitive and affordable rates. Their *"hook"* is their ability to shop all the major companies to get you the best possible offer. To the average consumer looking for life insurance, that seems like a really good deal. Chances are, they probably don't know that you can offer the same service locally, while providing *"world class"* customer service. There is no doubt that your clients would prefer to buy their life and annuity products from you, and not a stranger on the other end of an 800-telephone number. Remember what the commercial client said...." *You didn't tell me"*. Creating an email informing your clients that you can provide the same shopping service as the two aforementioned firms is an example of a product email. If they don't know, you cannot help them!

Life insurance products have changed dramatically over the past 37 years. The first universal life product was introduced in 1979 by E.F Hutton Life. Prior to that, our choices were more simple: term insurance or whole life insurance. In 1984, Thomas Wattererson[15] wrote in the Christian Science Monitor: *"It's been five years since E.F. Hutton tried to cut down the confusion over whether to buy whole-life or term insurance by introducing the first "universal life" policy. Since then, over 100 companies-many of which said they would never do it-have brought out their own versions of universal life.*

---

[15] Watterson, Thomas, *"Universal life, now 5 years old, still prompts insurance questions"*, Christian Science Monitor, April 1984

One of the byproducts of this half-decade of insurance advancement has been more confusion.

Universal life was supposed to be the life insurance industry's answer to recommendations that consumers avoid whole-life policies, with their 3 and 4 percent returns and high early-year premiums, in favor of much cheaper term insurance. The money saved on lower policies, it was argued, could be invested at a much higher return elsewhere. "Buy term and invest the rest" in a "side fund" became the catch phrase among "smart" insurance advisors."

Thirty-two years after Mr. Watterson's article, we have a better and less confusing understanding of universal life. When universal life was first introduced the side fund rate of return was in the 13 percent range. Since then, the rates have consistently declined. Many whole life policy holders were convinced to surrender their policies for universal life. In many cases, the agents did not properly explain the positive and negative aspects of the universal life product. In fact, we were all told by the so called *"financial experts"* that we would never see rates drop below 10 percent in our lifetime.

With rates as high as 13 percent, clients were shown universal life illustrations with no further premium payments or future payments for only a few years. That is, if the rate of interest on the policy remained at 13 percent. What many agents forgot to tell the client was, that if rates went down, more premiums would be required to keep the policy cash value growing or even to keep the policy in force.

Universal life is a tremendous product with the flexibility to adapt to the needs of the policyholder. Unfortunately, many policyholders never understood how the product functions and did not monitor the policy's performance on an annual basis. By not doing so, many universal policies have either lapsed or are in sad shape, not providing the coverage as initially projected.

Offering a policy review email is an example of category two, product and concept marketing. By reviewing a client's current life insurance portfolio, we can assess, not only their total life insurance needs, but determine if their current form of coverage (term, whole life, or universal life) is in line with their needs and desires.

I explained the history of universal life to demonstrate the necessity of policy reviews. Other emails offering both product and concept marketing discuss the changes that have taken place in the life insurance industry. For example, more current policies offer *"living benefits:"*. These benefits give the insured access to a portion of the death benefit while still living. Older life insurance policies only paid if you lived too long or died too soon. If you became ill and needed cash for medical expenses, your life insurance policy was of little help.

Successful businesses require careful planning, but planning for the death, disability, or retirement of an owner is often left undone. If proper planning is not done, a business could fail or result in a bankruptcy. A business planning email is an example of concept marketing.

You can see the different marketing approaches used to communicate within each category. You can also see that many of the concept and product emails crossover into each other's category. That's where proper filtering comes in as we create customized marketing campaigns based upon our *"Readiness Assessment Survey"* and *"Business Plan"* for every agency.

Once the marketing list is uploaded to our marketing department and the email schedule is established, we customize each email reflecting the agency's logo. Although we are conducting all email campaigns from our servers, your client recipients will recognize the communications coming directly from the agency.

Metrics are important. As we execute our overall marketing campaigns, it is important to analyze the results. In addition to directing the agency's email campaign, we will provide the agency with up to the minute data, including real-time data and daily reports, tracking opens, clicks, and other indicators of client interest.

CHAPTER 14

Total Risk Analysis

Property/Casualty risks *plus* Human Asset Risks = *Total Risk Analysis*. TRA is the reagent that drives the AgencyMaxx marketing system. Although discussed in a previous chapter comparing the different approaches used to make small sales verses large sales, TRA is worthy of additional mention because of its potential impact on an agency's profitability.

Insuring human asset risks is a voluntary process. Insuring most property/casualty risks is a required process. We cannot open the doors to our business unless we have purchased liability insurance, worker's compensation insurance, errors and omission insurance, etc. We cannot drive our car unless we have auto insurance or even get a mortgage without homeowner's coverage.

We purchase these insurance products, not only because they make sense, but because they are required. When you really think about it, we would not have a business, a car, or a mortgage, if not for us, personally.

Let's take the example of Jim Edwards, the owner JME, Inc., a small office supply company. Jim's company delivered office supplies to other businesses within a 50-mile radius of his warehouse location. One day, one of Jim's drivers called in sick and Jim had to take over the route. Unfortunately, Jim was involved in an accident and died that fateful day.

Jim had taken care of all the property/casualty risks that could affect JME, Inc., but was never approached by his agent about his human asset risks. Jim Edwards left a widowed wife and three small children. He did not have any personal or business life insurance.

JME, Inc., closed its doors soon after Jim's death. Jim's wife was able to sell JME's client list to a competitor at a fraction of its value. Ten employees of JME, Inc. lost their jobs.

JME, Inc. was Jim Edwards. He was the driving force behind the company and its most valuable asset. Without him, there was no JME. If his property/casualty agent had only taken a few minutes to discuss TRA, Jim may have understood the importance of the human asset risks he faced.

We have all known someone that died prematurely, leaving behind a family and/or a business.

Most large sales are made to commercial clients. Being able to explain, in a short three-minute presentation, the necessity of insuring human asset risks, will substantially increase your revenue.

One of the first things I learned about selling life insurance is that a sale will never be consummated unless you disturb the client. The clients must realize they face risks that could potentially devastate their family and/or business. Once they understand the importance of addressing these critical risk areas, they will follow your lead in providing the proper coverages.

The commercial and personal TRA presentations are the two most powerful arrows in your quiver. They are designed to help stimulate discussion about sensitive issues, with no hard-sell tactics or discussion of insurance products. Both presentations are designed to allow the clients to decide the appropriate next steps to take in handling the human asset risks they face.

We suggest your agents commit both presentations to memory. Once presented, your internal financial services specialist can take over the fact-finding interview or the agent can provide a red carpet (recommended) introduction to the financial services specialist.

If your agency does not have an internal life and annuity specialist, and you want to participate in the AgencyMaxx program, we suggest you consider working with one of our Certified AgencyMaxx Advisors. More details about working with an AgencyMaxx Advisor will be presented in a later chapter.

CHAPTER 15

A Powerful Suite of Marketing Resources

Although we described TRA as the backbone of the AgencyMaxx marketing system, driving your largest sales, it's on only one part of the overall program. Every agency will write large cases, either due to their proactive TRA approach, or reactively by being in the right place at the right time.

Our goal is to generate consistent production. To do so, we must utilize all the tools provided by the AgencyMaxx or AgencyLite systems.

As we study each agency's *"Readiness Assessment Survey"* and break down the demographics of their clientele, we keep in mind that the insurance consumer is constantly morphing. The dynamic nature of insurance marketing requires us to study the past, work in the present, and plan for the future.

Denise Garth[16]   recently wrote an article in Advisor Magazine entitled *"The Rise of the New Insurance Consumer, Are you ready for them?"* Ms. Garth is Senior Vice President of Marketing at Majesco. Majesco provides technology solutions,

---

[16] Garth, Denise, *"The Rise of the New Insurance Customer"*, Advisor Magazine, November 2016

products and services for the insurance industry across all lines of business – Property & Casualty, Life, Annuity, Health, Pensions, and Group & Worksite benefits insurance. Ms. Garth suggests that the entire insurance industry is being reframised. *"The unprecedented converging trends of people, technology and market boundaries outlined in our Future Trends: A Seismic Shift Underway report highlights how they are disrupting and redefining the world, its industries and its businesses – including insurance, Insurers, MGA's, reinsurers, and others must embrace this shift by understanding changes at play and accept that everything we have known about insurance was good for yesterday, but not good enough for today or tomorrow.*

The large differences between the generations on many aspects of the insurance experience highlight that established insurance companies were built for the two older generations, the Baby Boomer and Silent generations, which are declining in size and revenue power. In contrast, the two younger generations, Gen Z and Millennials (and increasing Gen X) have different experiences and behaviors that are at the core of why insurers need to redefine and reinvent themselves. Loyalty is now influenced by how well insurers meet their needs and expectations for products, engagement, and value."

Everything you just read applies, not only to the insurance companies, but to all of us, MGA's, NMO's, IMO's, BGA's, agencies, and agents. If you think it's "business as usual" it's time to rethink about the future of your agency and its ability to survive in our everchanging world of insurance marketing.

Most property/casualty agency websites that offer financial services (life and annuity) products, place the information behind a few screens that are difficult to find. When you do arrive, what you get is a very generic description of life and annuity products. If they offer a quote page, it's a lengthy form to be completed by the client and submitted back to the agency. That old-school process just doesn't cut it today.

If you're going to take the necessary steps to succeed, so eloquently expressed by Ms. Garth, then you must move forward at full speed. Filling out a form to get a quote a few days later just doesn't meet the needs and expectations of the customer for the next 10-20 years or the needs and expectations of those customers from the past 10-20 years.

Chances are you accepted these web pages from the firm that developed your site. Furthermore, the site was designed to market property/casualty products. The financial services part is nothing more than an afterthought or filler!

CHAPTER 16

Life Insurance Quoting Tools

To comply with Ms. Garth's recommendations, we must determine exactly how to meet the needs and expectations for products, engagement and value. Let's start with the property/casualty agency's website.

We all have a website, but just how effective is it in meeting the needs of our clients? Let's talk products first. As agents, we have little control over product development. On the life side, companies have done a good job in keeping their portfolios contemporary. The issues we face are communicative. Let me explain. If one of your millennial clients accessed your website and was interested in life insurance, what would they find? If you have the quintessential site as I described above, they would find very rudimentary information about the various forms of life insurance. This basic information may be tabbed under personal coverage, or possible benefits. Either way, chances are it will not be easy to navigate. Once you get there, you may possibly be directed to the *"Request a Quote"* page. All you know so far is that there are various types of life insurance, and term insurance is the most cost effective product for short (temporary) term needs.

Next, you check out the form and are not sure you want to provide all the requested information. You are also not sure how much life insurance you need, what kind, or for how long.

When discussing your website with your AgencyMaxx consultant, the first thing we suggest is creating life insurance visibility. Most websites have a series of tabs on their cover page. All we need to do is add a tab for life insurance. Now, when the client goes to your website and may be interested in life insurance information, he is immediately directed to the life insurance tab. Here's where it all changes. Behind the tab is a term insurance quoting tool. No more filling out a long request form. The client, without disclosing any personal information can fill in some basic information and receive a term quote on the spot. The quotes provided are from the most competitive and well known life insurance companies.

The quotes detail four underwriting classifications, based upon the health of the client. In addition, there is a needs analysis tool, as well as a detailed explanation of the underwriting guidelines. The client now has a good understanding of his needs, his underwriting classification, the product, and the cost of the coverage.

Next, the client is asked if he would like the quote emailed to him. If the answer is yes, the client and the agency receive a copy of the quote. The client now has the option to proceed to the application request form.

The short request application form asks the client's name, gender, address, and home or cell telephone number.

We cannot stress enough how consumer friendly the term quote tool is. The agent just needs to direct his clients to the tool. When an application request form is submitted, the client determined the amount of life insurance, created the quote, shopped for coverage, selected the carrier, and even provided information about himself, taking the giant first step to purchasing life insurance.

All research indicates that more and more insurance sales are taking place on the internet. The term quoting engine is the first tool created for the consumer and the agent to work either collaboratively or alone on the internet.

You no longer need to visit your client to work together. You can use a conference tool to work together or you can direct your client to your interactive banner on your website or to your microsite.

<u>Dropping the Ticket</u>

Now that your client has decided to purchase life insurance, what happens next? There is another tool, built exclusively for the agent called *"Drop Ticket"*. Here's how it works: All licensed agents in the agency register for the program through one of The Bollinger Companies' websites. To complete the registration, we require the agent to fax his signature to us.

The agent now calls his client that has requested the application form and reviews the quote. One of the tools provided to the agent in the program is a *"Health Analyzer"*. Although the client has read the underwriting requirements, it is always helpful if the agent reviews the client's health information through the *"Health Analyzer"* to confirm the possible underwriting classification.

The agent now submits the information into his *"Drop Ticket Quote Engine"*. Multiple quotes will appear. Next to the respective company quote is a red, amber, or green light. Based upon the health information provided, the program determines which companies will offer the most competitive premium. Better yet, if the light is amber or red, simply scrolling the mouse over the light will explain the reason the client should not proceed with that company.

The agent is now ready to proceed to a brief application request page. He asks the client some basic questions and drops the ticket. The entire process takes less than twenty minutes. The client never has to leave his home or office. The entire process is completed over the phone.

After the brief interview, the agent informs the client that he will be receiving a call from a vendor to complete the underwriting requirements. When that is complete, the policy is issued and emailed to the agent. It's that easy.

Back to Ms. Garth's checklist. Have we met the client's needs and expectations for product? Yes. The quoting tool and microsite are more detailed about the different types of life insurance. Additionally, when the agent contacts the client, he can explain the products in more detail and answer any questions posed by the client. Have we met the client's needs and expectations for engagement? Yes. By providing a state of the art quoting tool online and following up with a brief interview, we simplified the entire process. Have we met the client's needs and expectations for value? Yes. We have taken all the necessary steps to confirm the most appropriate underwriting classification and cost effective premium.

By adding an accessible life insurance quoting tool and microsite to your website, we have made it possible for you to engage your clients on their terms. Utilizing the *"Drop Ticket"* completes the process, creating client loyalty from Baby Boomers to Millennials.

Professional Backroom Consultants

Before I get into the AgencyMaxx Advisor Program, let me discuss the obligations an IMO or BGA has to the advisors they service. At The Bollinger Companies, we present ourselves as *"consultative intermediaries."* Although we are 100% wholesale, our highly-qualified Sales Vice Presidents are constantly educating our advisor sales force regarding new products, sales concepts, and industry updates. In addition, we are regularly working with our advisors to analyze and compare existing portfolios, so they can help their valued clients make informed decisions.

Working with our advisors, however, is only a small part of the duties of a Sales Vice President. In addition to marketing skills, each SVP must possess the necessary skills to communicate effectively with underwriters and carrier employees.

To successfully fulfill their fiduciary role, we have looked to hire individuals that have experience on both the carrier and brokerage side of the business. By doing so, our SVP's have a perspective quite different from many of our competitors. Having worked on both sides of the business provides us with a competitive advantage. Or course, not all our SVP's have corporate experience. If not, we regularly mentor them on how to most efficiently work with home office employees. By doing so, we have been able to place 75% of our submitted life premium and speed up the issue time for all products.

Before selecting a BGA, I suggest you request in depth information regarding their structure, their support system, and the backgrounds of their key contact employees. Are they just intermediaries or are they qualified consultative intermediaries? Doing a little homework upfront can make a huge financial difference down the road.

Let's look at the red flags you may encounter when interviewing prospective BGA's:

- <u>Compensation</u> – Remember the old rule of thumb,*"you get what you pay for."* In the financial services BGA world, most of us are aligned with one, or possibly multiple national marketing organizations. In general, that means many of us receive the exact same compensation from most carriers. Many carriers provide compensation guidelines for our contracted advisors.

   These guidelines are necessary so that an advisor can be contracted and paid directly from the carrier and to also discourage the outright buying of business by any BGA.

   If a BGA offers you the highest direct contract and then agrees to pay you an override on top of that, or tells you that they will pay you all but a minor percentage of their compensation, chances are you should head in the opposite direction. Obviously, that's a good indication they are in the volume business and not the service business. Working with a BGA that provides the highest quality of backroom service and knowledge, will ultimately put more money in your pocket than working with the highest bidder.

The next thing to lookout for is the BGA that offers to pay you directly. In essence, that means the BGA is licensing you under their contract. As such, the BGA owns the business and all the renewals. Although you are licensed with the writing companies, you have absolutely no ownership or vesting in the business you write.

Several years ago, when stand-alone long term care policies were the hot item, there was a BGA working with reps at Prudential Securities. He provided an agreement with the Broker/Dealer offering a first-year percentage of commissionable premium and a renewal percentage of premium. Sounds like a reasonable agreement at first, but when the third-year premiums were paid by the clients of the Prudential advisors, the BGA did not share any of the renewal compensation.

It seems as if the sly BGA's agreement with Prudential Securities offered a singular renewal, not renewals. Therefore, the BGA made all Prudential advisors sub-producers under his contract. The agreement agreed to pay one renewal to Prudential and nothing more. The BGA owned all the business and realized a healthy 15% renewal on all the business written by the advisors after the second year.

Most BGA's are reputable and more than fair to the advisors working with them; however, make sure you don't settle for anything less than a direct contract with the respective insurance company. That way, you are assured of a ten-year vested contract.

Many insurance companies heap first year compensation and do not pay any renewal commissions on term products. By heaping you receive as much as ten percent more first year commission and forego any renewal compensation. This compensation approach is common for term products but not so for permanent policies.

Don't hesitate to ask your BGA if the term insurance products they sell pay commission on policy fees. Quite often, companies have competitive term rates but exclude compensation on the policy fee that can be as much as $100. If you're selling a small death benefit term policy and encounter a hefty (non-commissionable) policy fee, be prepared to receive a small commission.

- <u>Conversion</u> – Although term insurance is the easiest form of insurance to understand, we feel it is necessary to go further with our advisors to educate them regarding the options, or lack thereof, available to their clients that purchase term policies.

  All term products are not created equal. Although all ten-year term policies will pay a death benefit if the client dies within the ten-year period, the similarity ends there. It is important to know if the respective company is offering your client any conversion options. How many years does the client have to convert the term policy into a permanent policy and does the company restrict the conversion to a single or only a few products in their portfolio. Some companies offer conversion options but only to one contract designed to address adverse selection. Always ask your BGA about the conversion options, including timeframe, age, and permanent policy availability.

All life insurance companies reserve the right to modify their conversion options at any time. All you can do is understand the available options when your client purchases a term contract.

I've shared a few key items with you that are important when selecting and working with a BGA. Don't be lured by commission alone and do your homework before committing to anyone. Most life insurance companies will allow advisors to contract through multiple BGA's. Not only does that create healthy competition but affords you flexibility. There are, however, some BGA's that will ask you to sign their own agreement, locking you into a long-term relationship. I suggest you look elsewhere if presented with such an agreement.

There is, however, a difference between a locked in agreement and the respective BGA's *"Business Associate"* agreement. To be compliant, a reputable BGA will request you sign a *"Business Associate"* agreement.

CHAPTER 18

Certified AgencyMaxx Advisors

One of, or perhaps the most inhibiting factor holding back many property/casualty agencies from committing to a financial services cross-marketing program, is their lack of life and annuity product knowledge. To many agencies, the program makes great sense until it comes time to follow up on the leads.

Going back to my discussion of the horror stories described in the first chapter, you may be quite hesitant to bring in a producer to market financial services. If you choose to establish your own internal department, you are assuming substantial financial risk and entering an area of marketing somewhat foreign to you. Many agencies have tried this approach, some successfully and some unsuccessfully.

Establishing your own Financial Services Department or separate Corporation may ultimately be the answer, but not initially prudent or feasible.

As you enter this additional marketing arena, it is most important to maintain a sense of equanimity. Contracting an outside agent to work your financial services leads is a potential solution. But, here again, *"Caveat Emptor."* Let the buyer beware: the principle that the seller of a product or service cannot be held responsible for its quality unless it is guaranteed in a warranty.

Enter the Certified AgencyMaxx Advisor. Quite often, the financial services advisor is as ignorant about the property/casualty business as you are about the financial services business. That's why so many of the half-baked arrangements I have seen over the years, never got out of the oven. Either the property/casualty agency was not happy with the sales tactics of the life producer, or the life producer was not satisfied with the leads provided by the property/casualty agent. Almost every time I make an AgencyMaxx presentation to a property/casualty principal, I hear some rendition of the same old story. I had a life guy and it didn't work.

If an agency is interested in adding an outside consultant to market the leads generated by the AgencyMaxx program, we recommend taking advantage of our Certified AgencyMaxx Advisor Program.

Prior to a life and annuity advisor becoming a Certified AgencyMaxx Advisor, he or she must pass our initial vetting process. Once we are satisfied that the advisor has the necessary advanced knowledge, sales skills, available allocated time, and personality to work with the most sophisticated commercial lines agencies, we invite them to participate in our AgencyMaxx Certification program. In our initial Certification program, we vetted over 73 advisors and only invited 13 to participate.

The Program

The Certification program is a four-step process. Over a period of one month. We get to know our students just like a teacher would in any classroom. By conducting regular training sessions, we systematically address the most important aspects of the AgencyMaxx Marketing Program.

Training Step One

- Who is the property/casualty agent and agency?
  - Personal Lines
    - Homeowners
    - Auto
  - Commercial Lines
    - Business Accounts
  - Specialty Lines including E&S
    - Admitted & Non-Admitted Markets
    - Definition of Markets and Statement of Diligent Effort
  - Mix of business percentage and total premium
    - The 5% Cross-Marketing Rule of Thumb
  - Mentality
    - Proactive vs. Reactive
      - CSR's
        - CSR Programs
          - Travelers, Aetna, Hartford
    - Required coverages
      - Auto, Home, Business
    - Voluntary coverages
      - Benefits (define)
        - Group health and life
        - Payroll Deduction

- o Individual Life, DI, Health, Annuity, Asset-Based LTC
- ■ Focal Points
  - Risk Analysis
    - o Loss Ratios, etc. (Empirical Data)
- ■ Financial
  - Contingencies
    - o 2004 Class Action Marsh and Mac lawsuit
      - ■ Elliot Spitzer – NY Attorney General
    - o Loss of Revenue
      - ■ Lower commissions
      - ■ Soft market
      - ■ Consolidation
      - ■ Competition
        - Direct writers
        - Internet (Personal Lines Auto)
- ■ Generalized Perception of Financial Services Advisor
  - Aggressive
  - Product Driven
  - Disruptive
  - Unprofessional
  - Slick
  - Gorilla in a suit
  - One step above a used car salesman
- ■ History
  - Brought in a life producer

- o No book
- o Stole my accounts
- o Caused me to lose business
- o Just doesn't work
  - ▪ Jargon and Lexicon
    - • Markets
    - • Renewals
    - • Hard/soft market
- o How do we find them?
  - ▪ Big I
  - ▪ PIA
  - ▪ Yellow Pages
  - ▪ Referrals (friends, neighbors, business associates)
  - ▪ Ask every business owner you know, including clients

The purpose of Step 1 training is to familiarize the advisor with the workings of a property/casualty agency and have a frank discussion of the roadblocks encountered when approaching an agency.

Training Step Two

- • How to approach the property/casualty agency
  - o AgencyMaxx email teaser campaign
    - ▪ The Bollinger Companies will create an AgencyMaxx email campaign to P/C agencies within the advisor's respective marketing territory.

- All leads will be passed through to our AgencyMaxx advisors.
  - Direct contact
    - The Bollinger Companies will share our email marketing list to afford direct contact within the advisor's marketing territory.
  - Identify and Certification
    - The Bollinger Companies will make available identification business cards to provide you with our Certified AgencyMaxx Advisor banner for your respective business card.
  - Initial Contact
    - The Bollinger Companies will provide sample scripts of introduction to the property/casualty principal.
    - The initial meeting should be relatively brief, introducing the benefits of the AgencyMaxx program and its unique features. The initial meeting is merely the "dangling of a carrot" in front of qualified agencies.
    - Presentation scripts will be provided, stressing the revenue opportunities and exclusive availability of the Program.
  - Follow-up Meeting
    - After the initial meeting, a second meeting should be immediately scheduled. The second meeting should be scheduled for one hour in duration.
    - We strongly suggest the second meeting be coordinated with The Bollinger Companies as

the presenters. In the presentation, we will discuss our 35-year experience within the P/C world, and explain in detail, the reasons why our Program is guaranteed to be successful.

- Certified AgencyMaxx advisors should coordinate an online meeting, presented by Marlin Bollinger, with every potential agency.
- During the online meeting, we will present our *"Total Risk Analysis"* approach to both personal and commercial lines clients, as well as providing a review and more details about the AgencyMaxx program.

The purpose of Step Two training is to assist the advisor in approaching qualified property/casualty agencies.

Training Step Three

- The Process
  - Selecting Prospective Agencies
    - The AgencyMaxx program requires considerable effort. Your time (advisor) and our time and effort are valuable resources. Therefore, selecting the right agencies in which to invest those resources is of key importance to you, The Bollinger Group, and to the success of the Program. To ensure proper agency selection, agencies should be measured by the pre-qualification guidelines:
      - Minimum premium all lines - $800,000+

- CRM – preferably Applied Systems – Epic or other
- Access to small businesses, professionals, and consumers with multi-line needs
- The agency should demonstrate:
  - Adaptability and an open-minded attitude
  - Sound management practices
  - Growth potential
  - A willingness to commit to the AgencyMaxx program
  - Willingness to participate in a *"Readiness Assessment"* evaluation – designed to determine the agency's financial soundness, organizational stability, and the ability to support the AgencyMaxx program
  - A willingness to execute our agreements
    - Consulting Agreement – designed to protect the P/C agency with strong ownership and non-piracy clauses
    - Confidentiality & Security Agreement - uploading of the agency's marketing list
    - Business Associate Agreement - HIIPA required
- The Marketing Plan
  - Success requires a written marketing plan. It should be jointly developed by the P/C agency,

the AgencyMaxx advisor, and The Bollinger Companies.

- o A solid marketing plan starts with stating where you want to go by establishing objectives:
  - What is to be achieved
  - How much is to be achieved
  - When will it be achieved
- o Our goal should be to develop customized strategies with each agency based upon the defined objectives.
- o The marketing plan should be comprehensive but as simple as possible.

The purpose of Step Three training is to assure that all parties are committed to the AgencyMaxx program and prepared to execute the marketing plan. In addition, we provide powerful agreements defining the role of every party. In the agreements, we offer security for all uploaded marketing lists as well as providing ownership, non-piracy, and commission split clauses for the protection of the P/C agency and the AgencyMaxx advisor.

Training Step Four

- Let's get the show on the road
  - o Six Steps to Success
    - Review the marketing steps from TAP – The Alliance Program
    - Make sure all advisors understand and can recite the *"Human Asset Risk Analysis"* for both personal and commercial lines.
  - o Sales Tools

- Review all sales tools available in the AgencyMaxx program.
- Review all features of The Bollinger Group and MarketMaxx websites.

- Backup
  - All AgencyMaxx advisors and participating AgencyMaxx agencies will have access to their appointed consulting team at The Bollinger Companies. Each team will consist of:
    - Dedicated Case Managers
    - A Life and DI Sales Vice President
    - An Annuity, Final Expense, and Asset-Based LTC Sales Vice President
    - Consultative services with The Bollinger Companies Marketing Vice President
    - All Bollinger Companies quote engines and websites
    - AgencyMaxx consultative services with Marlin Bollinger
    - Access to three senior level underwriters

Training Step Four is a review of the essential elements required of the AgencyMaxx advisor to achieve success (Human Asset Risk Analysis), as well as a review of all the services and programs.

By properly training and vetting all Certified AgencyMaxx Advisors, we have eliminated the *"Caveat Emptor"* when considering using an external agent to follow up on your leads.

CHAPTER 19

AgencyLite

Not all agencies are able to participate in the AgencyMaxx program, even though they may have a strong interest. There are several reasons for not adopting the entire AgencyMaxx program; however, the most common are lack of a Certified AgencyMaxx advisor in your geographic area, a desire to adopt only parts of the Program, or your agency does not meet the minimum qualification for AgencyMaxx. For agencies in this category, we offer AgencyLite.

AgencyLite offers many of the same highly successful parts of AgencyMaxx sans the turnkey email marketing program and the services of a Certified AgencyMaxx Advisor.

Regardless of where you are located or the size of your agency, we'll help you get the ball rolling in financial services cross- marketing with an assortment of successful tools that are easy to implement and simple to administer.

With AgencyLite, any agency, anywhere, can get started in cross-marketing in just a few short weeks. The Bollinger Companies will offer our complete portfolio of services, absolutely free of charge:

- Term quote engine for your website
- Exclusive product distribution opportunities
- The Bollinger Group Drop Ticket
- Exclusive webinar training
- Email marketing scripts
- Comprehensive backroom consulting

20/20

When someone refers to 20/20, we normally think of visual acuity. I think of the model property/casualty agency in 2020, just three years from the publishing date of this book. I wonder if the regional property/casualty agencies or the national property/casualty marketing organizations will have the business acuity to be keenly aware of the necessary changes to grow their respective firms.

Although there are some insurance carriers, agencies, and brokers that are exceptions, many have little to show for the many years of optimization they practiced. For example, from 1955 to 2006, the U.S. property/casualty industry had a return on equity (ROE) below the average for all U.S. industries more than 87% of the time.[17]

Fiserv, a provider of financial services technology to insurance companies and banks, published a white paper entitled "Driving Organic Growth: 5 Steps to Profitable Cross-Selling".[18]

---

[17] "Insurance 2020, Now what? Exploring initiatives for innovation", IBM Global Business Services, 2009

[18] Curry Pelot, Chief Information Officer, Intelligence Solutions for Fiserv

Cross-selling is critical because, if done properly, it achieves the following 5 goals:

1. **It's cheaper than acquisition.** It's 8-10 times more costly to acquire new customers than to sell additional products to ones you already have.
2. **It improves retention.** Dramatically. On average, a customer with just one product will stay for about 18 months. By adding just one more product, you extend that relationship (and income) to four years.
3. **It increases wallet share.** Wallet share is how much of a customer's assets are held at the same institution.
4. **It broadens your profit base.** A lot of customers add very little to the bottom line. Cross-selling can bring diversity and strength to the group you rely on the most.
5. **It's a "now" opportunity.** The dynamic nature of the entire insurance industry constantly creates a now opportunity.

Regional property/casualty agencies are the ones that face the biggest risk of losing their most profitable clients to the national full service P/C agencies, who dominate the market.

In response, some property/casualty agency managers want their agency to be viewed as having the capabilities to meet all of the client's insurance needs: P/C, life, disability income, long term care and group medical. A limited number of agencies have created in-house life and benefits groups in an attempt to make their operations seamless and a complete resource for their P/C clients.

Marlin Bollinger

Commercial agencies work with corporate executives, and corporate executives need solutions to both their business and personal coverage requirements. These two are oftentimes highly correlated. Property casualty agencies are a great source of clients, many of whom have complex asset protection and wealth preservation needs.[19]

Regional property/casualty agencies are currently faced with the greatest level of competition they have ever experienced. For them, 20/20 is critical and essential for survival.

AgencyMaxx can, and will provide profitable, cost effective cross-selling solutions for those agencies and national marketing organizations that have the vision and desire to commit to overcome their history of sluggishness. What will your visual acuity (20/20) be in 2020?

---

[19] Peter Klein, Property/Casualty 360, June 2013

Printed in the United States
By Bookmasters